Everything You Need to Know About

THE DANGERS OF HAZING

Hazing can occur anywhere—whether you're a new student in high school or a new employee at the local fire station.

Everything You Need to Know About

THE DANGERS OF HAZING

Jay Schleifer

THE ROSEN PUBLISHING GROUP, INC.
NEW YORK

Published in 1996 by The Rosen Publishing Group, Inc.
29 East 21st Street, New York, NY 10010

First Edition

Manufactured in the United States of America

Library of Congress Cataloging-in-Publication Data

Schleifer, Jay.
    Everything you need to know about hazing / Jay Schleifer. — 1st ed.
        p.   cm. — (The need to know library)
    Includes bibliographical references and index.
    ISBN 0-8239-2217-0
    1. Hazing—United States—Juvenile literature.   I. Title.
II. Series.
LB3609.S323   1995
371.8′1—dc20   95-9031
                                                                        CIP
                                                                        AC

Contents

Introduction: Brian's Story   7

1. Hazing: Always There and Everywhere   11

2. The Three Types of Hazing   17

3. School Daze, School Haze   24

4. How Many Hazed? How Many Hurt?   31

5. Eileen Stevens's Private War   36

6. Gang Hazing   44

7. Hazing and YOU!   50

   Glossary — *Explaining New Words*   58

   Where to Get Information   60

   For Further Reading   62

   Index   63

Hazing is used to show power and control over another person.

Introduction
Brian's Story

*F*rom the day he started high school, sixteen-year-old Brian had dreamed of making the football team. It was one of the top squads in the state and had just made the playoffs. Now Brian's dream had come true. He'd been named backup quarterback. And all he wanted was to make some winning plays to help his new teammates.

Unfortunately, that's not all his teammates wanted of him. One night, ten of them jumped Brian in a shower. They dragged him, kicking and screaming, to a nearby towel rack. Then, stretching two-inch-wide tape tight across his bare skin, they hung him up to dry.

About twenty other students had been invited to watch the "show." One was the girl Brian had taken to the school's Homecoming dance. "Having her see me like that was as bad as the pain," Brian said later.

When it was over, Brian complained to school officials. To his surprise, the school refused to suspend anyone, though they did make the team members say they were sorry. Brian simply had received the welcome given to new members of the *team, it was explained. "We don't favor hazing," said the football coach. "But this has always gone on in school locker rooms."*

Brian took his case to the county school board. They took action, canceling the team's trip to the playoffs.

Suddenly Brian was the most hated student in school. "He should have taken it like a man," fellow students said, "not gone squealing to the school board." Now, when Brian walks down the hall, few students talk to him. Instead, they punch him hard in the back as he goes by.

What happened to Brian was an act of *hazing*. That's the word used when a group makes someone go through a painful or embarrassing ordeal, often as a test of how much they want to join that group, or as a "welcome" when they do. It's a practice that can turn upside down normal ideas of what is right and wrong, lawful and unlawful. Brian's story shows how much that is the case.

The law says that dragging a person off and holding him by force is *kidnapping*. Wrapping a person with tape against his will is a form of *assault*. Both are serious crimes that lead to terms in jail.

The young men who hazed Brian were not charged with any crimes, however. In fact, the authorities made excuses for them. The person who ended up being punished most was Brian himself—for reporting the crimes.

Why is hazing an exception to the basic idea that people should not hurt other people? Why do authorities sometimes protect hazers? Why do the victims seldom complain—and why are they hated if they do? How can people who wouldn't step on even an ant when alone become brutal and hurtful when they act within a group? This book takes a closer look at the longtime, worldwide custom of hazing. Let's start with its history.

Members of fraternities and sororities usually live together in large houses on or near campus.

Chapter 1

Hazing: Always There and Everywhere

When Brian's coach said hazing "has always gone on," he probably didn't know how right he was. The Smithsonian Institution has researched the history of hazing. It found that in one form or another, hazing has been part of life for thousands of years.

Many cultures, the Smithsonian noted, have required some form of painful ordeal when young people reached their teen years and became full members of a tribe. Certain Native American societies stuck young men with plant needles until it hurt too much to move. Others hung young girls from the roofs of their huts for up to four months. Young people have been beaten, cut up, and left in the wilderness—all in the name of testing their readiness for adulthood.

In societies more like our own, hazing has a long history as a part of student life. In the 1600s,

England's famous Oxford University put its freshmen through something called "salting and tucking." First, the students' chins were nicked with razor blades until they bled. Then the young people were made to gulp salt water. The salt ran painfully into their wounds as the drink dribbled down their chins.

Even the German religious leader Martin Luther approved of hazing. Freshmen attending his school in Germany were forced to wear devil ears to class while upperclassmen taunted them. The way to end the agony was to agree to be dunked in a barrel of wine.

When the freshmen complained, Luther had a ready answer—that hazing prepared them for life. "You'll be bothered by employers, shopkeepers, even your spouses all your days! This test is only a symbol of what is to come."

Hazing is a worldwide custom. In France, it's called a *brimade*. Some Canadians know it as *gummering*. In England, it's been called *fagging*. And wherever it exists, it is part of many of the activities of life.

Hazing at Work

Many workplaces include some special "treatment" when a new employee joins the group. Sometimes it's as mild as having to carry the boss's luggage around on business trips. But at

Incoming freshmen and new students are prime targets for acts of hazing by older students.

one U.S. store chain, new employees have had cream pies thrown at them.

Workers whose jobs are to protect others from harm are not protected from hazing. A Wisconsin firefighter suffered major injury when he was run through nonstop drills as a way of welcoming him aboard. A California police officer was handcuffed to a jail cell and sprayed with water when she joined the force.

Clubs that Haze

Social groups such as the Masons and Elks are known for holding secret ceremonies and giving coded hand signs. But some clubs also haze. One has been known for blanket-tossing new members in the air. Serious injuries have occurred when victims didn't land properly. Another club beat new members with paddles while forcing them to climb over spinning barrels. A third forced newcomers to dip their hands into goo they were told was animal waste. It was actually mashed food.

The Moose Lodge used to haze but no longer does. The practice was outlawed when two men died in a new member "welcoming" ceremony.

Boot Camp Blues

If hazing had official colors, they'd likely be Army green and Air Force or Navy blue. Anyone who has gone through "boot camp," where soldiers get their first training, knows all about hazing.

Tough sergeants haze newcomers from the moment they get off the bus. Insults and name-calling are the mild part. The harder part is physical punishment. A trainee may have to do hundreds of push–ups or run miles in the rain just because someone doesn't like the look on his face. And that is even though extreme punishment without good reason is a crime under armed forces law.

Some in the military see hazing as a way of toughening recruits against the far worse treatment handed out by an enemy in battle. But military hazing goes on even in peacetime.

Sports Hazing

In sports, hazing has long been part of the game. From the little leagues to the majors, rookie athletes have been razzed by their teammates— and their managers.

Sometimes this "horseplay" can get ugly. Heads are shaved. Mouths are stuffed with tobacco and hot peppers. Players are made to exercise until they fall down and pass out. And a wrestling team in Oklahoma gives its rookies a new coat of paint. "They strip you down, rub bubble gum into your hair and armpits, then spray-paint your body," one wrestler told police.

In pro sports there is less hazing because team owners have cracked down on it. They don't want their million-dollar athletes damaged.

Hazing is often used in the military to "toughen" recruits.

Chapter 2

The Three Types of Hazing

If you call it creative to find ways of making people miserable, then hazers are true artists. There's no end to the stunts they've been able to design. But looked at broadly, the acts of hazers fall into three basic categories:

Messing with the Mind

Mental hazing seldom results in physical harm. It's designed to make the victim look and feel ridiculous and to give the hazers and onlookers a laugh at the victim's expense. Some examples of mental hazing are:

- Strange clothing, hats, and signs
  It's natural for young people to want to appear before their friends in the right clothes, hairstyle, and makeup. Hazers know that, and they use clothing to make victims suffer.

Victims are paraded around in diapers, dog collars, or barrels. Male students are forced to wear dresses, high heels, and women's underwear. In one common stunt, the victim has to "streak"—run naked—through a dorm or restroom used by the opposite sex. Victims are also made to wear signs such as "I'm a No-Brainer" or "Kick Me—Please!"

- Slavery

  Slavery was supposed to have ended with the Civil War, but hazers have found a way to bring it back. Newcomers seeking to join a group are named slaves to an existing member, who becomes the master. The slave must do any job the master orders, even if it's as dirty and unreasonable as cleaning a grimy floor with a toothbrush. Each newcomer must also behave like a slave, bowing to the master and speaking only with permission and with eyes cast down.

- Begging/Quests

  Activities in this group move hazing to the great outdoors. Victims are made to grovel to strangers on the street and beg, often asking for nonsense items, and often wearing oddball clothing. Male students from a Kansas college were dressed in women's clothes and sent on a quest for "ostrich eggs" and "bat wings." The young men felt silly when their trip began but worse when it ended. Police stopped their truck for a traffic offense. It just happened that the officers were being filmed for a TV police show, and the young men—one wearing a ballet dancer's tutu—ended up on national television as the unwilling stars of *Real Stories of the Highway Patrol.*

Terror Hazing

A long step beyond mental hazing are stunts designed to fill victims with fear and terror. In fact, terror hazing can come close to what secret police organizations such as the World War II German Gestapo or the Russian KGB used on their victims.

A typical example is the "buzz saw game." The would-be member of the group is shown a power saw, then blindfolded. As he is held down, the shrieking, buzzing saw is moved closer and closer until he screams in fear of losing parts of his body. The saw is moved away only at the last second.

In another terror stunt, the victim is tied to a rock with a rope, and the rock is tossed off a rooftop. The victim knows that when the rope pulls tight, his body will follow. The rope has been secretly cut so that it will fall away harmlessly, but nobody tells the victim that.

Hazers have thrown their victims in ditches the victims had been told were graves; told them they'd be drowned in "wells" that turned out to be only inches deep; and tricked them into drinking from bottles marked *Poison*. The bottles held only soft drinks.

Sometimes terror hazing gets out of control. A New Jersey student was told to dig a fake grave and lie in it. The walls collapsed on the student. The fake grave suddenly, horribly, became a real one.

Physical Hazing

This last category, physical hazing, has resulted in serious injury and death.

- Binge, Starve, Stay Awake

It's common for young people away at school for the first time to eat too much or too little, or perhaps to do some drinking and stay up too late. But hazers use food, drink, and lack of sleep as weapons. Would-be joiners of some organizations have had food rammed down their throats until their body systems failed. In one group, a tube called a "beer bong" was stuffed down a victim's throat and beer poured in. The tube stayed in until the victim threw up.

Other groups make the price of entry going without food for days at a time. And food hazing doesn't have to involve eating: A Texas group pelted newcomers with raw eggs for 72 straight hours. Some 800 *dozen* eggs were thrown.

During many of these ordeals, the victims are

Acts of hazing can make a person feel confused, hurt, and embarrassed.

kept awake by endless screaming and taunting. The hazers work in shifts. They get their sleep—even though the victims don't.

• Beyond the Limit

Exercise is good for the body. *Overexercise* is not. To test the strength and will of would-be members, hazers often call for endless running, push-ups, or weight lifting. It's common to run these drills outdoors in freezing cold or midday heat, putting even more stress on the body.

Another test is to force the victim into dangerous behavior. Victims have had to climb rock walls without training or safety equipment; to hang onto the roofs of moving cars; and to

lie down in the middle of fast-moving traffic.
• Sticks and Stones . . . and Paddles

There's nothing creative about a beating, but that's what some hazers favor.

A fraternity at a suburban New York high school welcomed new members with what it called the "Atomic Bomb." One young man, just 14 at the time, was made to stand with arms held high. Eight "brothers" then slammed their fists into him as hard as they could. When doctors first examined the student, they thought they'd have to remove his spleen.

It's common for new members to have to "run the gauntlet," a tunnel formed by existing members lined up from one end of a room to the other. As the victim runs through the tunnel, he or she finds its walls are lined with pounding fists and kicking feet.

Many groups deliver their beatings with an old-fashioned paddle. But this particular paddle is said to be made of a magical wood that "carries the victim's old life away" as it's whacked against his body. This leaves him "reborn" as a member of the group: a member with welts and bruises, that is.

Paddles are often marked with the name or symbol of the group. These markings can be seen on the victim's skin after the beating.

In a recent twist on the idea, some groups brand their members, just as ranchers mark

One form of physical hazing includes a beating with an old-fashioned paddle.

their cattle. A bent wire hanger is heated red-hot and used to burn the group's symbol into the skin.

No matter how the hazing is carried out, it always sends the victim the same basic message: We have power over you—your mind, your body, your life. If you want to join our group, you'll have to accept that.

Chapter 3

School Daze, School Haze

School is a series of new beginnings: You enter a new grade each year, and a new school every few years. Along the way, clubs and organizations beckon for you to join them. Since hazing often happens when starting something new, this makes school a fertile ground for hazing.

It begins in grade school, where older students gang up on incoming kindergarteners. This has nothing to do with joining a club; it's simply to show power. "Kids will taunt another child," says Dr. Sheldon Zaplow, a child–raising expert. "They'll trip him or shove him against walls, spread lies about him, or circle him like a pack of wolves."

In junior high, hazing often occurs if the new student is different in any way. He or she may wear a different style of clothing, speak poor English, or be handicapped.

"Junior high youngsters often are unsure of how accepted they are by others," says Zaplow. "One way to feel better about yourself is to make someone else feel worse." Another expert, Mark Helmer, adds, "In junior high, the only way some kids think they can be *in* is by pushing someone else *out*."

High School Horror Stories

These behaviors graduate to a new level in high school. That's when they change from simple acts of meanness to the official acts of organizations. They may even be part of the school's traditions.

In many high schools, for example, it's almost a right for seniors to torment incoming freshmen. In fact, if you're wearing a freshman beanie you might as well have a target pinned to your head.

"When freshmen walk through 'Jock Hall' at our school," reports Trish Flock-Johnson, a Minnesota teacher, "upperclassmen place a dollar bill on the floor. When freshmen bend over to pick it up, they're harassed until the bill is handed over."

And then there's the dreaded "swirlie." It has to do with a freshman's head and a certain bathroom fixture.

High school clubs sometimes conduct hazing in a way that mirrors the club's interest. One group with an interest in farming calls new members "greenhands" and makes them dip their hands or arms in green paint. This is pretty mild. But at one chapter, new members were spread-eagled and run into the school's flagpole. "I did that to my best friend," says a former chapter member. "I didn't mean to hurt him, but that's life."

But high schoolers don't need to join an organized group to go along with what they know is wrong just to feel accepted. Amy Minter, a Minnesota student, recalls the "Friday Club" at her high school. Every Friday, the group's custom was to haze in the parking lot before class. "Many went along just to get in with that crowd," she says.

"Brace!"

Some of America's finest high schools and colleges are military schools. Because they operate like army bases, these schools have traditions of hazing. In fact, for "plebes," as freshmen are called, hazing can be a way of life.

From morning roll call to lights out, plebes face endless insults. Whenever ordered by an upperclassman, they have to "brace"—stand in a stiff, frozen position, sometimes for long periods of time. Plebes receive unkind nicknames. And the slightest breach of the rules can bring punishment from fellow cadets.

One student was hazed because he couldn't close his thumb properly in a salute. "He caught a lot of heat for that," one hazer said later. "But it's

More than 200,000 college students face hazing every year. Many of them are Greek organizations such as sororities.

important to salute properly." Another was hung by his fingers over an upward-pointing sword.

How do plebes feel about hazing? "It's almost like a prisoner-of-war camp here," said one young cadet at a famed school. "We all suffer together," added another. "That's how we form friendships."

But the father of another cadet noticed a different result. He wrote a letter to the school's commander: "I'd like to know what changed my son from a happy person to a tired, bitter, and confused one."

Not every military academy hazes to the same degree, and some hazers are severely punished or expelled. But as in the armed forces, hazing will probably always be a part of the cadet's way of life.

Welcome to College!

Stop anyone on the street and ask where hazing happens most, and you're likely to be told: *college fraternities and sororities.*

These groups of students live together on or near campus, usually in a large private house owned by the group. Male groups are "frats." If the members are women, it's a sorority.

Such groups are usually named with Greek letters, such as Sigma, Delta, Omega, or Tau, and called Greek organizations. They hold parties called "rushes" at which freshmen get a sales talk about joining up. Those who decide to try out are "pledges." They remain so until voted in or out by the members. The pledging period can last from a few weeks to six or more months.

During pledging, would-be members have to prove they're worthy of the group. Some tasks are mild: Pledges raise money for charity, or they do community cleanups. But others include hazing, usually in the form of being forced to do ridiculous stunts, endure beatings, or drink too much. The hazing gets strongest during "Hell Week" or "Hell Night," the last phase of pledging. That's often when the tragedies happen.

A recent addition to the Greek scene is the forming of high school fraternities and sororities. They're not national organizations, but they resemble the ways of the college groups—including hazing.

Pledges may be forced to perform exhausting or embarrassing tasks as part of the hazing process.

Chapter 4

How Many Hazed? How Many Hurt?

It's hard to find accurate numbers on how many students face hazing. One survey found that about half of the college Greek groups haze. That means more than 200,000 students go through the process each year. There are no figures on how many young people are hazed in high schools or other groups.

It's just as difficult to learn how many young people die from *violent* hazing. Studies show an average of one or two deaths a year, but the figure may be low. Deaths reported as suicides or even car accidents may be connected with hazing. After all, a car crash that kills a drunken student looks the same whether the driver was forced to drink or just wanted to.

Those who survive hazing tell their stories, but often no one will back them up. Hazing tragedies happen in rooms filled with students; yet when the

You should not have to suffer just to join an organization in which you are interested.

police ask for witnesses, they're often told that nobody has seen anything.

Sometimes the injuries are to the victim's feelings. When they are, it's harder to see them. And sometimes the effects don't show up for years. Then, just as abused children grow up and abuse their own youngsters, hazing victims become hazers. They do to others what was done to them.

Those in Favor . . .

If hazing causes such problems, why haven't school officials, parents, and youth group leaders joined together to stamp it out? Because many of these leaders think that—so long as it's kept in control—there's nothing wrong with the idea of making young people "suffer a bit" to get what they want. Here are the points often made in favor of hazing:

- *Builds loyalty and friendship.* Those who go through an ordeal together often form a lifelong bond. They gain from these friendships long after the discomfort they felt is forgotten.
- *Builds respect for the organization.* The more new members have to "pay" to enter a group, the harder they're likely to work for it once they get in. On the other hand, supporters of hazing say that those who refuse to be hazed probably would have made poor members. Hazing weeds

out those who don't care enough about the group to suffer for it.

- *Brings status to group members.* Outsiders know which groups are the hardest and most demanding to enter. When you're part of an "in" organization, people treat you with special respect.
- *Teaches teamwork.* In any group effort, some members may disagree with the team's actions. But the power in a group comes from working together. When members go along with hazing, *even if they don't believe in it*, they've learned a lesson in teamwork.
- *Toughens the spirit.* As Martin Luther said, during our entire lives we deal with pressure— pushy bosses; too much work; things that don't happen as they should. A little pressure during our school years helps us to learn to deal with these bothers later.
- *Tradition.* Some groups have hazed new members in the same ways for one hundred years or more. When current members repeat these "time-honored" acts, they feel linked to the past. Besides, the acts must be right and good because they've lasted so long.

One South Carolina newspaper summed it up when it opposed an antihazing law: "Some hazing is not only *not* dangerous, it's downright fun! Anyway, students don't have to undergo hazing because they don't have to join groups that haze."

. . . And Those Against

Others believe hazing is wrong, no matter how mild or how much "fun" it may be. Here's a summary of their arguments:

- *It's simply wrong to make people suffer.* No one should be forced to go through an ordeal just to join an organization. It harms the victim and the hazer alike, making both into harder and less caring people. If schools teach that it's all right to hurt others, the members of the next generation will be no kinder than those of the last.
- *Lets the "bad apples" rule the barrel.* In any large group, there are always a few individuals who *enjoy* making others miserable. From the class bully to the evil leader of a foreign nation, such people have always existed—the "bad apples" in the human barrel. Because they're "talented" at hazing, such people gain power in the group. Hazing lets "the beast within us" run wild.
- *Teaches the* wrong *kind of group behavior.* It's true that everyone on a team needs to pull in the same direction. But those against hazing believe it's a member's duty to speak out when it's the wrong direction.
- *Time for a change.* Hazing may be a tradition, but that doesn't mean it should continue. Bad traditions should be destroyed.

Chapter 5

Eileen Stevens's Private War

*I*n the fall of 1978, Eileen Stevens sent her son Chuck off to a well-respected college in upstate New York. Five months later, she brought him home—in a coffin. Chuck had died during a fraternity hazing.

On "Hell Night," Chuck's would-be "brothers" had handed him a bottle of liquor, a six-pack of beer, and a bottle of wine. Then they'd locked him in the trunk of a car. Chuck was told that when he'd finished all the booze, he could get out of the trunk—and into the fraternity.

After a while, the hazers began to worry. There was no signal from the trunk. When they opened it, Chuck was out cold.

Nobody called a doctor. Instead, the brothers dumped him on a bed to sleep it off. Hours later, Chuck was dead—killed by alcohol poisoning.

When Eileen reached the college, everyone felt bad but no one would take the blame. The stunt had

Pledges are often forced to drink large amounts of alcohol to show their loyalty to the fraternity.

been done many times and had never hurt anyone else, school and fraternity officials told Eileen. Two other young men had gone through it that same night, and they were fine. What happened to Chuck was just an accident. These things happen. They said they were sorry.

The fraternity was barred from school activities for a while, but no one was arrested or thrown out of school. When Eileen checked a few years later, all records of the case had somehow disappeared.

Speaking Out

Someone else might have swallowed the pain

and gone on, but not Eileen. She vowed to work so that no other parent would lose a child to hazing. She wrote to lawmakers. She appeared on TV shows and told her story to magazines. And she started the Committee to Halt Useless College Killings—CHUCK, for short—which keeps track of the harm that hazing causes. When newspaper reporters need information on hazing, they call CHUCK.

Eileen is one of several leaders in the antihazing movement. A similar group called CHORUS operated for a time in Massachusetts and focused on high school hazing. And several leaders have worked hard to stop hazing in many fraternities.

One result of this work has been antihazing laws. When Eileen's son died, fewer than eighteen states outlawed hazing. Now, at least thirty-eight states have passed laws, though each describes hazing differently. The Illinois law, for example, bans "any amusement done [to hold up] any student to ridicule." Other states, such as New York, ban activities that put a victim in danger. But the New York law doesn't say anything about simply making fun of someone.

Most antihazing laws carry fines of less than a thousand dollars and call for short jail time, a few months at most. Some allow hazers to work in the community instead of going to jail. The regular laws against kidnapping, assault, and the like are used to punish hazers in the most serious cases.

Eileen Stevens formed a committee called CHUCK— Committee to Halt Useless College Killings—after her son died during fraternity hazing.

Antihazing leaders are glad the laws exist, but they still worry about how much they are observed. "Whether the laws are enforced remains to be seen," says Eileen Stevens.

Do Victims *Want* to be Hazed?

Even where there is no law, many organizations have outlawed hazing. Their top officials are against it. But it is often difficult to get local group leaders to use those rules with their members.

One excuse that's made for not clamping down on hazing is that the victims "willingly go along with it." "It's something they *want* to do to prove themselves," the hazers say.

"Not so," says Irving Janis, who studies mental stress in young people. "Students go along because they want to be accepted." "When you're new in a school," adds 19-year-old Oregon student Deborah Miller, "you do anything, no matter how stupid, to get in with the 'right' group."

"Groupthink"

If groups didn't exist, neither would hazing. That's because people do things in groups that they'd never do alone.

Examples of this are plentiful: Soldiers get the bravery to face a powerful enemy by having their buddies with them. People who are angry at some new law but are doing nothing about it get together on a street. Suddenly they turn into an organized protest. Otherwise honest people loot stores after an earthquake because they see others doing it. And otherwise gentle students haze in the most violent ways for the same reason.

This weird change in behavior has a name: It's called "groupthink," or in severe cases, "mob behavior."

Victims, too, are bitten by the groupthink bug. Normally, they'd fight back if someone tried to hurt them. But when a group is behind the act, "might makes right." The lone victim meekly accepts whatever the group dishes out.

Alternatives to Hazing

Hazing has been a constant part of student life since before the days of Martin Luther. But lately there are some signs that this may be changing. The change is part of a movement by students to get serious about the business of learning and to do away with sources of pressure that stand in the way, such as the fear and misery caused by hazing.

- Organizations are simply giving up hazing. Some groups have ended pledging altogether and admit anyone who applies. Others have renamed pledges "associate members" and treat them like full members, although the newcomers still need to be voted on before they gain full membership.

- More organizations are banning alcohol from parties and ceremonies, or they're banning the use of group money to buy alcohol. Alcohol abuse has been a major cause of hazing tragedies.

- Groups that choose to keep pledging are changing from hurtful to helpful ways. "Hell Week" is now "Help Week" at some schools, and "I-(Inspiration) Week" at others. During this special time, pledges may prove themselves by doing such tasks as building housing for people in need. Some groups conduct special classes on how members can help each other to improve as people.

- One sorority now has a "reverse hazing" program, in which current members wait on the pledges. Senior members bring the newcomers fresh flowers each day and serve them breakfast in bed.

For a long time, groups believed that if someone refused to be hazed, he or she would have made a poor member anyway. Now that view has been turned upside down. People who refuse to be hazed tend to be smart young men and women who think for and believe in themselves, the kind of people any group would want. "We started to realize that the kind of people we wanted were not pledging us because of our hazing," says one group leader.

Cracking Down!

These days, when hazing happens, authorities are more likely to crack down. Schools are suspending and expelling hazers. Sports leagues are kicking out teams that haze their players. And the police are filing serious charges more often when a tragedy does occur. When a Missouri pledge recently died from a severe beating, the organization was expelled from the school, and seven members were charged with manslaughter.

There are many reasons for this. Anytime a student is hurt, the school's insurance costs may rise. With the end of the baby boom, there are fewer young people to enroll. Schools are working to rid themselves of anything that stands in the way. And more and more group leaders are beginning to think hazing is just wrong.

"We've been too easy on hazers," says Fred Kershner, a national fraternity official. "It's criminal. It breaks national rules and laws. It's so bad I don't know why we try to be nice to those who do it."

Chapter 6

Gang Hazing

Another form of hazing you need to know about is street gang hazing.

Gangs are far from being just another kind of youth group, even though they may call themselves "clubs" or "crews." Other groups may get wild at times, but they basically believe in society and its laws. Most gang members feel left out of society. Breaking the law to get what they want is no problem at all for them.

Gangs make their money by stealing, threatening shopkeepers, and selling drugs; they fight anyone who tries to muscle onto their "turf" (even if it's just a street corner); and they beat and kill without a second thought to prove they mean business. These aims shape the way gangs find and "jump in" new members.

Possible gang members, or wanna-bes, are hazed through a series of tests, such as stealing from another person.

Tests of Skill

In a bizarre twist on fraternity "rush" parties, many gangs actually hold meetings for young "wanna-bes," who are usually in their early teens and known to present gang members from school or the neighborhood. The youngsters get a sales pitch on how being in the gang will bring them money, respect, drugs, and sex. They're also told that by joining the gang they'll be helping to protect their families and their neighborhood.

The gangs want members they can depend on, so it's rare that anyone is actually forced to join—unless the gang is threatened by another gang. Then, like an army at war, they begin to "draft" new members. Those who refuse to go along are threatened with broken bones or injury to their families.

The hazing itself is done as a series of tests. Each test checks out a new member on the skills gangs depend on. Can a new person fight well? How strong is he? Will he run if threatened? To find out, a tough member will pick a fight with the newcomer and test his skills in battle until both are bleeding.

Is the new person afraid of the law? *Is he working for the law?* The gang will send the new member out on a mugging, beating, or minor theft, then wait. If others who went along on the crime are questioned or arrested, it's a sign the new person is a police informer. If so, he may never be heard from again.

When a wanna-be becomes a full gang member, a tattoo is sometimes cut or burned into his skin.

Even if the new member is "cool," this test has a second purpose: The youngster has now taken part in a crime. If he ever tries to quit, the gang tells him that they'll tip off the police and have him arrested.

Getting Tattoos

When the wanna-be passes these trials he becomes "made," a full member. He is given a gang name and often has tattoos cut or burned into his skin. He often gets something else—a beating by all the members as a "welcome aboard."

Young women have their own version of this process, even though many gangs don't allow them full membership. Females are prized for sex and as carriers of drugs and stolen goods, in the belief that the police are less likely to search them.

Female wanna-bes have their own hazing to face, sometimes described as a "short punch and hair-pulling ceremony." In some gangs, a new female will be told to have sex with several male members to prove her loyalty.

If gangs are active in your area, never treat them as anything other than what they are: dangerous criminals, as willing to kill you if ordered to do so as to shake your hand. It doesn't matter if a gang member was a friend of yours before jumping in. He or she is now playing by different rules in a different world. If a member puts an old friendship before an order from the gang's leaders, he risks punishment or death. Chicago gang member Robert "Yummy" Sandifer killed a 14-year-old girl he'd known in the neighborhood because his leaders ordered it. The gang then killed Yummy to keep him from talking, although he was just 11 years old. Other gangsters have killed members of their own families on orders from the group.

As soon as someone becomes a member of a street gang, his or her loyalty belongs *first* to that gang.

What if They Want ME?

Gangs look for new members with a history of fighting and petty theft. That's the kind of "talent" they depend on. If you don't have it, they probably don't want you any more than you want them.

If you are asked, don't try to deal with it yourself. Seek help from your parents or school or police authorities. Gangs respect power. And you'll need some serious adult help behind you if you plan to take them on.

Chapter 7

Hazing and YOU!

It is possible that at some point in your school career you're going to meet hazing face-to-face. A group of students may try to make your life miserable. Or you may be asked to pay a price in pride or even blood to join a group or take part in an activity that means a lot to you.

You may already be a member of a group that hazes. In that case, you'll be asked to stand by and watch or even take part in acts that make fun of or harm others. What will you do? How will you react?

If it Hurts, It Must Be Hazing

First, decide if what's happening is actually hazing. That's fairly easy to figure out if new members are being beaten, force-fed liquor, or buried in a ditch.

But what if the activity is no more than name-calling? Or being asked to dress in funny clothes and stand on a street corner? There are plenty of innocent actions in which people just trade wisecracks or fool around.

The key question is this: *Is the person being harmed mentally or physically by what's being done, even if those who are doing it think it's just fun?*

One way to know is to watch those undergoing the treatment. Are they in pain or sick in any way, or in any kind of danger? If not in physical danger, do they seem comfortable with what's going on? Are they laughing with the group? Or are they forcing a smile, while inwardly gritting their teeth?

Another test is to imagine that the act is being done to *you*. How would you feel? If the answer is "not very good," the act probably meets the definition of hazing.

But it still may not be *hazing*.

Is the action coming from someone in authority, such as a teacher or team manager? If so, it may be a proper punishment for breaking rules. Hazing is a serious charge! Before you make it, you must know what's really going on.

What to Do

If it is hazing, what do you want to do about it?

Again, there's an easy answer—and a harder one.

In cases where someone's life or health is at risk, your duty is clear: *You should make an immediate report to authorities, or be on the phone dialing 9-1-1!*

This may not only save someone's life, but help keep your group from getting into bigger trouble than it already is. It may not be pleasant for your friends to face hazing charges, but it's better than facing kidnapping, assault, or manslaughter.

If the person being hazed does *not* seem sick or in danger, your duty is still to stop it if you can. But keep these facts in mind: People who report acts of hazing are often not listened to or taken seriously by the authorities. It's possible that no one in the group will back up your story. *Even the victims may say that nothing happened because they still want to get into the group.*

Even if the authorities believe you, there's no guarantee that they'll take action. Officials may not want it known that such things happen in a school or club under their control for fear of losing their jobs or being sued.

At the same time, once the word gets out that you've broken the silence, you're likely to be treated like a traitor by the group.

A Better Answer

Nobody wants to be in that position. But there is a way out, and it's a way in which both the organization and the possible hazing victims come out ahead:

Work beforehand to end hazing abuses in your group.

If you feel something wrong is happening, chances are that other members feel the same way. Find out who they are and talk about hazing with them, one at a time.

Why one at a time? To get away from "groupthink." A person may say he or she favors hazing when everyone is doing it. But one on one, the person may be a lot less sure it's the right thing to do—and a lot easier to convince that it's not!

If enough members feel as you do, or you can convince enough to feel as you do, you may have the votes to elect new leaders or make new rules. Ask for a group meeting. If the number is small, you can at least agree to back each other in reporting abuses and telling what happened.

How to Report Hazing

First, talk to your parents. You need their support before going to anyone else, especially to officials. That's because the officials will probably call them in after a report is filed. Parents can also give you an adult's view of what's going on to make sure you're not getting in the way of a proper action.

If you're in grade school, junior high, or high school, report hazing problems to the school official who handles behavioral matters. High schools often have a vice principal in charge of discipline, or a dean of students. If that person can't be reached, drop a note to any teacher or other official. Top school officials do see hazing as an obstacle to learning. "We oppose hazing, and any practice in which one student abuses another, [and see it] as a breakdown in the positive attitude schools should have," says Dr. John Lammel of the National Association of Secondary School Principals.

If the only way you feel able to make a report is without giving your name, don't sign the note. The authorities need the facts more than they need your name.

College Hazing. This can be reported to the dean of students or, if a fraternity or sorority is involved, to the college's Greek Council.

Sports Hazing. After consulting your parents, talk first to the team coach or athletic director or adviser. If there's no action, you may need to contact the sports league the team plays in, or the city or state scholastic athletic association. Teams that haze can be suspended or tossed out of the game for good.

Employment Hazing. Workplace laws don't mention hazing, but they may forbid certain acts that happen in hazing. No one can call a person

If you are a victim of hazing and decide to report it, you'll be helping other possible victims—as well as yourself.

unkind names or treat them unfairly based on age, race, sex, or handicap, for example. That's called *discrimination*.

Health and safety laws require employers to provide good food and care if you live or are fed on the jobsite, and laws control the hours you can be required to work. Of course, the usual laws apply against physical force or cruelty.

Just as important, larger companies usually have strict rules on how managers can treat employees or how employees can behave toward each other. The penalty is usually loss of one's job.

If you think you're being hazed, report it to the department manager. If that does no good, talk to the personnel or human resources department at your location or at company headquarters. If the company refuses to take action or you feel you are being punished for reporting hazing, take the problem to your state labor department or the local office of the U.S. Department of Labor, or talk to a private attorney.

What to Report

Whomever you report to, you need the facts, *in writing*. These include:

- The date, time, and place the hazing happened
- The names or descriptions of hazers and victims, and of those watching
- *Exactly* what happened from start to finish

Your account should be written as soon as possible after the hazing. It should describe *only what you actually saw*, not what others have told you or what you think happened. If others are backing you, they too should write reports or sign yours.

Then get ready for a possible battle. Even the worst acts of hazing have their excusers. Milder acts have supporters. You may be told that things have always been done this way; that nobody minds but you; and that you're making trouble where there isn't any. At such times, remember that *hazing is against the rules of most national groups and against the law in dozens of states.*

You might also remember what antihazing leader Eileen Stevens tells the hundreds of groups she speaks to:

"I've heard all the excuses for hazing . . . that it builds friendship . . . respect . . . that it's a tradition. But you'll never make me believe there's anything good about hazing. You can build all those things through activities that are positive and useful. And you'll never get respect from people by hurting or embarrassing them. You have to earn it."

Before Joining

If you plan on joining a group, check them out first. Talk to current members and those who've left. Don't be afraid to ask if they haze new members. If they do, you might want to think about whether an organization that welcomes people in this manner is one you want to be part of.

In other words, are THEY good enough for YOU?

If not, *just say no.*

Glossary—*Explaining New Words*

assault Physical attack on a person; **battery** is the actual striking of that person.

binge To overeat or drink too much.

boot camp Military base at which recruits get their first training.

brace Stand rigidly at attention.

fraternity All-male group of students who often live together and agree to help each other during college and afterward.

gauntlet A tunnel formed by lines of people who hit and kick those running through. *Running the gauntlet* is a common form of hazing.

Greek organization Fraternity or sorority.

hazing To make someone do hurtful or ridiculous things, often to be allowed into a group or organization or to celebrate their joining.

Hell Night or **Hell Week** The end of the pledging period, when hazing often becomes severe.

initiation The act of bringing someone into an organization.

58   **jumping in** Joining a street gang.

kidnapping   The moving and holding of a person against his or her will.

manslaughter   The unlawful but unplanned killing of a person. (If a killing is planned, it's **murder**.)

ordeal   A difficult or painful experience.

paddle   A flat stick often used in hazings.

plebes   Freshmen students in a military academy.

pledge   Student who has applied to join a Greek organization.

rush   Party held for freshmen students by a Greek organization to entice them to join.

sorority   All-female group of students who often live together and help each other during college and afterward.

"swirlie"   Form of hazing in which a person's head is forced into a toilet bowl as it's being flushed.

wanna-be   Would-be member of a street gang.

Where to Get Information

On hazing in general:

Committee to Halt Useless College Killings
   (CHUCK)
P.O. Box 188
Sayville, NY 11782

Attention: Ms. Eileen Stevens

On your school's, group's, or team's policy on hazing:

- Your group's national or state headquarters
- Your team's league headquarters, or the state scholastic athletic association
- Your school administration or central school board

On your state's position on hazing or antihazing law

- Office of the State Attorney General
- Local police department

To find names and addresses of group headquarters, see the *Encyclopedia of Associations* at
most libraries.

Government agencies can be looked up in either
the state or local directory or the blue pages of
many phone books.

For Further Reading

Gardner, Sandra. *Street Gangs in America*. New York: Franklin Watts, 1992.

Gunn, E. P. "It's Time to Put an End to Fraternity Hazing." *Seventeen*, April 5, 1991.

Jankowski, Martin Sanchez. *Islands in the Street (Gangs)*. Berkeley, CA: University of California Press, 1991.

Newer, Hank. *Broken Pledges: The Deadly Rite of Hazing*. Atlanta, GA: Longstreet Press, 1990.

Plummer, William. "Fit to Be Tied: The Hazing Humiliation of a High School Athlete." *People*, December 13, 1993.

Index

A

alcohol abuse, 20, 42, 50
antihazing movement, 38–40
assault, 8, 52

B

beating, 22, 47
begging, 18–19
boot camp, 14
"brace," 26
brimade, 12
buzz saw game, 19

C

college, 28–29, 54
Committee to Halt Useless
    College Killings
    (CHUCK), 38

D

discrimination, 55

E

Elks club, 13

F

"fagging," 12
fraternities, 28–29, 36–37, 43,
    54
friendship, 33, 57

G

gangs, 44–49
    female, 48
Greek Council, 54
Greek organizations, 28–29
group behavior, 35

"groupthink," 40–41, 53
gummering, 12

H

hazing, 8, 31–35, 50–51
    alternatives to, 41–42
    college, 28–29, 36, 54
    gang, 44–49
    history of, 11–15
    mental, 17–19
    military, 14–15, 26, 28
    physical, 20–23
    reporting, 8, 52, 53–57
    school, 24–26, 54
    stopping, 43, 51–53
    terror, 19–20
    work, 12–13, 54
Hell Week/Night, 29, 36, 42
Help Week, 42
high school, 25–26, 29, 31,
    54

J

"jumping in," 44

K

kidnapping, 8, 52

L

laws, antihazing, 38–40, 56
    opposing, 34
loyalty, 33, 48

M

"made," becoming, 47
manslaughter, 52
Masons club, 13

military, 14–15
    schools, 26–28
mob behavior, 41
Moose Lodge, 14

O
overexercise, 21

P
paddle, 22
plebes, 28
pledges, 29, 41, 43
power, 23, 24, 49

Q
quests, 18–19

R
respect, 33, 46, 57
reverse hazing, 42
"run the gauntlet," 22
rushing, 28, 46

S
salting and tucking, 12
sex, 46, 48
slavery, 18
Smithsonian Institution, 11
sororities, 28–29, 42, 54
sports, 15, 54
status, gaining, 34
Stevens, Eileen, 36–40
"swirlie," 25

T
tattoos, 47
teamwork, building, 34
tradition, 34, 35, 57

U
U.S. Department of Labor, 56

W
"wanna-bes," 46, 47, 48

About the Author
Jay Schleifer has written more than forty nonfiction books for young readers. Raised in New York City, he has been a public school teacher and was the editor of *Know Your World Extra*, a national classroom publication which received several EdPress awards. Currently, Mr. Schleifer is a publishing company executive and resides in the Midwest.